What Does Light Do?

Alan Trussell-Cullen

Dominie Press, Inc.

Publisher: Christine Yuen
Series Editors: Adria F. Klein & Alan Trussell-Cullen
Editor: Bob Rowland
Designers: Gary Hamada & Lois Stanfield
Photographers: Superstock (pages 4, and 8); Simon Young (pages 10, 12, 14, 16, and 18)
Illustrator: Mike Lacey

Published by:

◕ Dominie Press, Inc.

1949 Kellogg Avenue
Carlsbad, California 92008 USA

www.dominie.com

ISBN 0-7685-0557-7

Printed in Singapore

11 12 V0ZF 14 13 12 11

Table of Contents

Light from the Sun 4

Light from Fire 6

Light from Electricity 8

Our Shadows 10

Shadow Puppets 12

We Need Light to See 14

Mirrors 16

Picture Glossary 20

Index 20

Where does light come from?

Most of our light comes from the sun.

We use fire
to make light, too.

We use electricity
to make light, too.

Light cannot pass through our bodies. That is why we have a shadow.

12

We made shadow puppets
with our hands.

Our eyes need light to see.

We see the light that
"bounces off" things.
We say it is reflected.

Shiny objects like mirrors reflect light best.

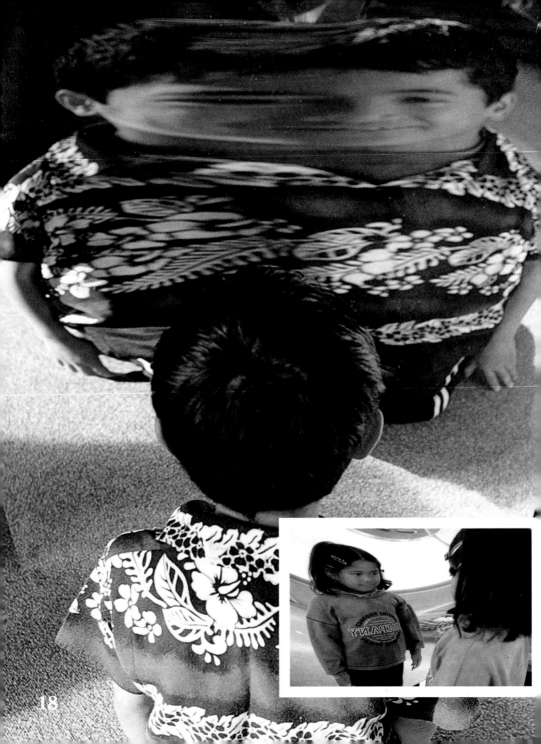

But watch out!

Mirrors can play tricks on us.

Picture Glossary

mirror:

shadow puppet:

shadows:

sun:

Index

electricity, 9

fire, 7

mirror(s), 17, 19

shadow(s), 11

shadow puppets, 13

sun, 5